Virtual Reality in Emergency Management

Evolving Disaster Response Practices

Table of Contents

Chapter 1. Introduction

In this enlightening Special Report, we peel back the curtains on one of technology's most thrilling advancements, Virtual Reality, and its impactful role in the realm of Emergency Management. Untangling the complex threads of this innovation for eager readers, we examine how it's revolutionizing disaster response practices globally. This report enlightens those working in disaster response and curious individuals alike, exploring captivating case studies, insightful expert commentary, and rich analyses. Any apprehensiveness about the technicality of the topic is quickly dissolved as we deliver the report in everyday language, easily digestible and thought-provoking. To be at the forefront of your awareness in emergency management tactics, you won't want to miss this Special Report – a comprehensive guide to the intersection of Virtual Reality and Emergency Management.

Chapter 2. The Dawn of Virtual Reality in Crisis Control

The first virtual reality headsets tentatively made their way into the market in the late 20th century, barely hinting at the potential that this technology could bring to the world of crisis control. Since then, we've seen an inspiring evolution, as this technology integrates itself within the emergency management realm, revolutionizing how we prepare for, respond to, and recover from disasters.

2.1. The Advent of Virtual Reality

The term "virtual reality" was first coined in the late 1980s, but the concept has been alive in science fiction literature for much longer. Early prototypes were miles away from what we now define as virtual reality, largely involving simple headsets and gloves for rudimentary movement tracking. However, these early days were crucial in validating the potential of immersive, three-dimensional experiences.

With advancements in technology also came evolutions in the virtual reality space. Refined motion sensors, improved display technologies, and advancements in software led to a more immersive, realistic VR experience. It wasn't until the tech revolution of the 21st century, however, that virtual reality found its footing in consumer technology, particularly for gaming and entertainment. It was only a matter of time before innovators started considering the potential applications of the technology elsewhere, such as emergency management.

2.2. Virtual Reality Meets Emergency Management

Recognizing the potential of virtual reality in crisis situations, researchers embarked on a journey of exploration, testing the limits of the technology and its applications in the field. In the early 2000s, a number of projects began tackling the concept of VR simulations for disaster response.

Specialized VR systems were developed, designed to create realistic, immersive scenarios of various disasters, from earthquakes to floods to fires. These scenarios served multiple purposes: they could be used for education and awareness, to help individuals understand how to act in such scenarios; as well as for training professionals in the field, enabling them to practice in a controlled environment before possibly facing a real disaster.

2.3. Training Through Simulation: A Practical Application

One of the most immediate areas where VR has had an impact in crisis control is in the training of emergency responders. It allows for the replication of scenarios too dangerous to practice in real life, or too costly to reproduce physically.

Firefighters, for instance, can wear VR headsets and be transported to a towering inferno, a situation too dangerous and unpredictable to be ethically recreated for a training exercise. Paramedics can be thrust into chaotic, crisis-ridden environments where they must triage effectively while under intense situational pressure.

These simulations are typically programmed with various parameters in mind, and can be adjusted to create different disaster scenarios. This ensures a thorough training experience that enhances readiness and effectiveness in the face of actual crises.

2.4. Advanced Disaster Preparedness

While the training benefits are obvious, VR also offers significant contributions to disaster preparedness. Communities can be placed within a virtual disaster scenario, allowing them to understand the potential severity of a situation and encouraging them to implement preventative measures.

Virtual reality can provide an immersive experience of an impending hurricane, for instance, and the aftermath it can potentially leave behind. This can be a powerful tool to persuade individuals to evacuate areas under threat, or to invest further in disaster-proofing their homes.

2.5. A Step into the Future: The Full Potential of VR in Crisis Control

While we've taken significant strides in the application of VR to crisis control, there's a wealth of untapped potential yet to explore. Future applications could include real-time disaster modeling, improved inter-agency collaboration tools in virtual environments, and AI-assisted disaster response training.

Despite the strides still to be made, we are witnessing the dawn of a new era in virtual reality applications in emergency management. As we continue to refine and evolve the technology, we can expect even more powerful impacts in disaster control and management. Virtual reality is no longer the stuff of science fiction—it's here, it's real and it's ready to make a significant difference in crisis control.

Chapter 3. Breaking Down Tech: Simplified Understanding of VR

To fully grasp the potential of Virtual Reality (VR) in Emergency Management, a clear and simple understanding of VR itself will first be furnished. This groundbreaking technology, capable of transforming static two-dimensional pictures into a dynamic and interactive three-dimensional environment, alters the way we perceive, interact with, or even reshape reality.

3.1. The Basics of Virtual Reality

The term Virtual Reality might sound fairly self-explanatory, referring to a 'virtual' or simulated version of 'reality.' However, it is anything but simple in its execution and impact. VR is a sensory experience that can include sight, touch, hearing, and increasingly, smell. Typically, it involves a user entering a digital environment through the aid of technology such as a VR headset or a similar device. Once in this environment, the user can interact with its elements, dictated by the level of immersion the VR system provides.

3.2. Levels of Immersion

Just as physical reality varies in its experiences, VR also has its degrees or levels of immersion:

1. Fully Immersive: In this mode, users are completely enveloped in the VR environment, experiencing a high level of realism. High-resolution visuals, surround-sound audio, and haptic feedback devices contribute to fully immersive VR. Examples include high-end systems like the Oculus Rift and HTC Vive.

2. Semi-Immersive: This level of immersion employs projection systems and large screens to provide users with a compelling VR experience, but with a lesser extent of user-system interaction compared to fully immersive VR. Flight simulation systems are common examples.

3. Non-Immersive: Characterized by a less immersive experience, this form of VR denotes situations where users still interact with a virtual environment but are fully aware of their physical reality. This includes computer games played on a desktop with a mouse and a keyboard.

3.3. VR Devices

Now to ponder the actual equipment enabling us to enter these virtual universes. Below are the three most common:

1. Head-Mounted Display (HMD): As the name suggests, these are devices worn on the head that present an immersive VR environment to the wearer. They are equipped with one or two screens, speakers, and numerous tracking sensors. High-end offerings like Oculus VR, PlayStation VR, and HTC Vive dominate this category.

2. VR Glasses and Goggles: These devices provide a similar experience to HMDs but are more compact, lightweight, and portable. They offer a semi-immersive experience, often used with drone operations or 3D simulations.

3. Cave Automatic Virtual Environments (CAVEs): These are room-sized VR environments where images are projected onto walls, floors, and ceilings, capable of stimulating an immersive experience. This technology is often found in blueprint simulations or archaeological expeditions.

3.4. Creating Virtual Environments

The magic of VR lies in the meticulously crafted environments that users interact with. These environments, composed of data-fed, digitized 3D models, are created through a multistage process:

1. Data Acquisition: The initial stage involves collecting comprehensive data, often achieved by using CAD software, 3D scanners, or photogrammetry.

2. 3D Modelling: This phase constructs digital 3D models using the data obtained.

3. User Interaction: Enabling a user to interact with the created 3D environment is the final step, facilitated by devices like VR headsets, gloves, joysticks, treadmills, etc.

3.5. VR and Its Immediacy

Arguably the most impressive feature of VR is its immediacy, or the real-time interaction offering users a sense of presence within the virtual world. This factor greatly enhances the immersion and realism of VR. To facilitate this real-time interaction, VR systems use two key components:

1. Tracking systems: These systems monitor a user's movement (head or body) and translate it into the VR environment to allow for real-time interaction and responsiveness.

2. Rendering software: This facilitates the swift generation of graphics in response to the user's movements, contributing to virtual environmental realism.

Virtual Reality, as a technology, is vast and brimming with possibilities. Complex in its executions, its spheres of impact stretch out into diverse sectors - from entertainment to education to emergency management and beyond. The above breakdown offers a simplified understanding of its mechanisms, making the complex accessible. This comprehension will pave the way for appreciating how VR – this uncanny combination of reality and illusion – can transform disaster management, up next in our exploration.

Chapter 4. Historical Review: Conventional Methods in Emergency Management

Emergency management has undergone several crucial changes over the past few decades, continually adapting to fit the needs of an ever-fluctuating global environment. By scrutinizing the predecessors of current disaster response protocols, we can better understand the novel opportunities offered by technologies like Virtual Reality.

4.1. Chronological Development of Methods

Pivotal to understanding the contribution of virtual reality to emergency management is tracing the evolution in the sector's responses to disasters and crises. The approach to emergency management has been largely chronological, starting with the reactive phase, transitioning to an emergency-oriented phase, then to an inclusive disaster management phase, and finally to the compounded emergency management phase.

The reactive phase was the earliest form of emergency management when responses were purely reactionary and often ad-hoc. Typically, a disaster occurred, leading to ad-lib and immediate reactions, without any systematic preparation or forethought. The emergency-oriented phase marked efforts towards a more organized approach, with organizations setting up emergency departments and creating mitigation plans to prevent or cushion the impact of disasters.

Next was the disaster management phase, which introduced an all-hazards approach. Here, in anticipation of potential disasters, plans went beyond mere emergency response to include recovery and mitigation strategies. This phase utilized knowledge and lessons gained from previous experiences to devise more efficient responses.

The present, advanced phase of compounded emergency management incorporates not only all the aspects of the earlier phases but also elements of disaster risk reduction and climate change adaptation. This phase champions a more holistic view of disaster management.

4.2. Emergency Management Stakeholders

Critical to the historical review of emergency response is the enlistment of prominent stakeholders in the progression of disaster management over the years. This evolution in strategies would not have been possible without the concerted efforts of these entities who continue to propel advancements in the field.

National and regional governments have played significant roles, responsible for enacting policies and ensuring their efficacy. Dedicated government agencies – such as FEMA in the US and corresponding structures in other countries – have been instrumental in managing country-wide initiatives.

Non-Governmental Organizations (NGOs) have also provided substantial contributions, particularly in regions where governmental infrastructure is lacking or inefficient. NGOs often lend a hand in crisis situations involving significant humanitarian efforts, taking charge of things like fundraising, volunteer coordination, and direct aid.

The UN and other supranational institutions have played memorable roles, particularly in the coordination and standardization of global efforts. Their comprehensive outreach has facilitated shared learning and resources across borders.

4.3. From Response to Resilience

A crucial shift in the historical journey of emergency management has been the evolution from response to resilience. The increased frequency and intensity of disasters led to a shift in the mindset of emergency management, from merely responding to disasters to developing resilience against them. This paradigm change encouraged a proactive rather than reactive perspective, prompting holistic preparation for disasters by considering potential risks and vulnerabilities in advance.

Key to this shift was the acknowledgement that disaster management needs to integrate with other sectors such as urban planning, environmental regulation, and infrastructure development. Such integration would enable communities to better prepare for, withstand, and recover from disasters.

Additionally, the recognition of communities' and individuals' roles in disaster response and resilience has transformed during this progression. Increasingly becoming more involved, civilians contribute by volunteering, donating, or even participating in decision-making processes. This inclusion has led to a more ground-up approach, supplementing traditional top-down methods.

4.4. Technology and Emergency Management

Another essential thread in the history of emergency management is the role technology has played in its ongoing evolution. With advancements in geospatial technology, organizations and governments are now able to better assess potential risks and disaster-prone areas. Through early warning systems, they provide alerts for impending disasters, allowing for timely evacuation or other preparatory measures.

Communication technologies have enhanced the ability to disseminate information rapidly and efficiently, crucial in emergency situations. Social media platforms, in particular, have revolutionized how agencies inform the public and liaise with one another.

Software and digital platforms have streamlined the coordination of efforts, allowing for more efficient use of resources. They have also provided a way to track and predict resources' needs as a disaster unfolds, helping to mitigate impact.

Simulation technologies have played a notable role in training and preparation. Simulated disaster scenarios have allowed first responders and crisis managers to practice responses, planning, and communication in a controlled environment, enhancing overall skills and preparedness.

In summary, the historical exploration of emergency management practices reveals a domain that has witnessed significant evolution. This development, marked by shifts from reaction to resilience, has been facilitated by technological advances and the proactive participation of a broad array of stakeholders. As we move forward, it's this cumulative wisdom that will inform the incorporation of virtual reality and other novel technologies into emergency management. Now, the question is how these new tools will further revolutionize this critical field for true disaster resilience.

Chapter 5. Case Study: VR in Firefighting and Rescue Operations

The pace at which technology has been advancing is astonishing – every day brings a new fleet of innovations, each more exciting than the last. Virtual Reality (VR), once viewed as a novelty for gamers, is now transforming how emergency services approach rescue operations, especially firefighting.

5.1. Firefighting and VR: The Unlikely Duo

Essentially, VR creates immersive simulation environments that look, feel, and even sound incredibly real. Fire departments across the globe are using this technology for training and improving the efficiency of their responses. VR allows firefighters to virtually experience a wide range of scenarios without the risks associated with live-fire exercises.

By allowing firefighters to acclimate to various emergencies in a secure environment, VR technology can reduce the risk involved in training and provide a more comprehensive understanding of fire dynamics. In essence, it permits firefighters to safely experience worst-case scenarios while learning how to best respond.

5.2. VR Firefighting Training in Action

Take West Midlands Fire Service (WMFS) in the UK, as an example. In a groundbreaking application of VR, WMFS developed an immersive

360-degree experience to improve fire safety. This experience simulates a house fire from the perspective of an individual trapped inside, showcasing how quickly the flames can spread and demonstrating the importance of fire safety measures.

Moreover, alongside training for house fires, firefighters can use VR for complex emergency situations, like high-rise building fires, hazardous material spills, or airplane crashes. Working within these simulations better prepares them for a diverse set of firefighting scenarios while also providing an opportunity for seasoned firefighters to refresh their skills or learn new approaches in a risk-free environment.

5.3. Handling the Hurdles: VR in Rescue Operations

VR applications aren't limited to training alone. They can facilitate rescue operations by helping analyze structures before entry, minimizing the potential risks involved. By creating a virtual model of a building, firefighters can get a better understanding of its layout, all while identifying potential hazards before they even step foot inside - a benefit seen as a game-changer by many in the firefighting community.

Case in point, the Fire Department of New York (FDNY) actively uses VR technology to virtually explore infrastructures and study building plans. By doing this, they can strategize before being dispatched, increasing their efficiency and safety during operations.

5.4. Feedback and Simulation: Learning From Mistakes

Key to this training and familiarization process is the ability to capture and analyze data. VR systems can provide invaluable feedback to firefighters, allowing them to review their actions and responses post-simulation. This feedback loop is vital for continuous learning and improvement. Responders get the opportunity to experiment with different decision-making pathways and then learn from any mistakes made during the process.

5.5. The Bigger Picture: Impact on Emergency Management

The integration of VR technology into firefighting and rescue operations not only promises to revolutionize how these services operate but also indicates a shift in how we approach disaster management as a whole. The adoption of VR provides a snapshot into the future of emergency response, demonstrating that technology can be leveraged for the greater good, mitigating risk, and potentially saving lives.

However, while VR's potential in firefighting and rescue is significant, it's important to keep in mind that it's a tool to supplement and not replace traditional hands-on training and experience.

5.6. Looking to the Future: VR and Beyond

While still perceived as avant-garde by many, VR technology is quickly becoming an industry standard. As it continues to develop, the only limit to its uses in firefighting and rescue operations will be how far our imagination takes us. The coming years will likely see more immersive VR applications within emergency management, leading to more intelligent decisions and, in turn, safer and more efficient rescue operations.

The future looks promising for VR in emergency management. From creating a safer training environment to providing crucial intel to rescuers during operations, it is clear that VR has begun transforming the way the firefighting community learns and reacts to emergencies. As the technology continues to evolve, its impact on firefighting and rescue operations will undoubtedly continue to blossom.

Surely, as we step into this new era of technological advancements, there will be hurdles to overcome. However, the potential benefits that VR brings with it in tackling these complex and high-pressure conditions are unparalleled. The innovations might be swift, but the outcomes – saving more lives and doing so more efficiently – make embracing VR a path worth pursuing for firefighting and rescue operations.

Chapter 6. Case Study: VR in Natural Disaster Preparedness

When considering disaster management, it is important to fully understand not only the material impact a catastrophe can have but also the most effective ways to prepare and respond. Today, we're diving deep into the compelling case of how Virtual Reality (VR) is being used in preparing for natural disasters, offering examples, expert analysis, and an in-depth study of this promising avenue.

6.1. The Uses and Benefits of VR

The introduction of VR practice scenarios into emergency management has many tangible benefits. Training exercises can be conducted in a controlled and safe environment, reducing the risk of physical injury. Scenarios can be easily repeated, allowing for the reinforcement of procedures and protocols until they become second nature.

Furthermore, each VR scenario can be varied and reshaped, encompassing not only a wide range of potential disaster situations but also differing environmental and geographical circumstances. This versatility amplifies the preparedness of emergency services and the public for dealing with natural disasters anywhere and in any form.

6.2. VR for Training First Responders

First responders are often subjected to dangerous circumstances for the first time during real-life emergencies. VR minimizes this problem by creating high-pressure environments akin to real life. The global VR in the training market is expected to reach $6.3 billion by 2022, a projection that signifies the gravity of this tool in the training sector.

An illustrative instance of this approach can be seen in the partnership between VR software company Pixo VR and the Sacramento Metropolitan Fire District. Together, they've formulated immersive, realistic 3D virtual reality simulations for first responder training. Trainees can learn to react to a variety of unexpected situations in a safe, controlled environment, reducing the gap between theory and practice.

6.3. VR for Public Safety Education

While first responders are undoubtedly a critical component of disaster response, public safety education and individual perception of risk can play a significant role in preventing disaster situations from escalating.

In Japan, a country frequently subjected to earthquakes, the Tokyo Metropolitan Government has made use of VR to simulate the experience of an earthquake to the public. This initiative takes participants through different levels, starting from the seism to the aftermath, all the while offering valuable information on how best to secure personal safety during an earthquake. By doing so, they not only raise awareness about the importance of disaster preparedness but also equip individuals with practical advice that could prove life-saving in the face of an actual event.

6.4. Evaluating VR Training Effectiveness

While the use of VR in disaster preparedness presents an appealing opportunity for enhanced training and public safety education, it is of equal importance to evaluate its effectiveness. One of the best ways to assess this is to compare the performance of those trained in traditional ways with those trained in VR.

A study conducted by the US Fire Administration indicates that VR-trained individuals responded better to real-world scenarios compared to their traditionally trained counterparts. The VR-trained firefighters were able to apply classroom theory to physical incidents, resulting in improved operational efficiency and reduced casualties.

6.5. Looking to the Future

As technology develops and becomes more affordable, the inclusion of VR into disaster management training is set to grow. The success of its application in earthquake-prone regions like Japan and for the training of emergency responders paints an optimistic picture of the scope of VR in this field.

Experts opine that even though the initial investment in VR technology may be steep, the long-term benefits and cost savings in terms of increased efficiency and reduced fatalities due to better training far outweigh the investment. Given this forecast, it's safe to predict that VR will play an increasingly pivotal role in disaster management preparations in the future.

By fully leveraging the capabilities of VR, we have the potential to augment disaster preparedness in entirely new ways - revolutionizing the approach to emergency training, enriching public safety education, and ultimately fostering a society that is better equipped to deal with the raging fury of nature.

Chapter 7. Bridging the Gap: Integrating VR into Current Emergency Management Systems

The integration of Virtual Reality (VR) into Emergency Management Systems (EMS) presents an exciting evolution in disaster response. As technology progresses, VR is gaining ground as a tool to transform and improve disaster management and emergency responses. This chapter explores how we can address the challenge of integrating VR into current disaster response systems, breaking down barriers and bridging gaps to innovate using this modern technology.

7.1. The Potential of VR in Disaster Management

Firstly, it's crucial to understand the immense potential of VR technology within disaster management. The most notable use is its highly realistic simulation capabilities, providing a chance to experience various hazardous scenarios without actual risk. Predictability is an essential aspect of emergency management, and VR allows us to forecast events, plan, and prepare accordingly.

Utilizing VR, emergency personnel can safely simulate threatening situations such as forest fires, earthquakes or floods. It offers an environment to practice efficient evacuation plans, test communication systems, and improve crisis decision-making capabilities. The immersive nature of VR helps spur emotional engagement, thus improving the retention and application of learned strategies.

7.2. Challenges in Integrating VR into EMS

While the potential benefits of integrating VR into EMS are vast, there are hurdles to its mass adoption. Perhaps the most significant challenge lies with its cost. Developing VR simulations demands considerable resources and is, as a result, expensive. The expense includes not only the VR hardware but the software and maintenance as well.

Moreover, there is a substantial technological learning curve for users. While some people may quickly master the nuances of VR technology, others, particularly older individuals, may find it more challenging. Training and educating the workforce is a necessary but time-consuming and costly process.

Access can also be a problem. Internet connectivity is a prerequisite for accessing VR technology. However, in many rural, remote, or underprivileged areas worldwide, obtaining a stable internet connection is still challenging.

While these barriers exist, they can certainly be surpassed. Further technological advancements and shifts in the perception of VR technology are likely to make the technology more accessible, affordable, and integrated into emergency management.

7.3. Building the VR Bridge: Steps for Successful Integration

Understanding the potential of VR and the challenges that come with its integration allows us to strategize a bridge-building plan that better marries VR to EMS.

Investment and Financial Planning

Recognizing the initial cost involved in VR integration is vital. Outside of the price tag on VR equipment and development costs, organizations must earmark funds for user training, continuous updates, and maintenance. Funding could come from government allocations, private sector contributions, or even crowdfunding initiatives.

Education and Training

Promoting user competency in VR is critical to successfully integrating the technology into EMS. Recognizing that a learning curve exists, implementing step-by-step training modules can help users become comfortable navigating VR platforms. Inviting technology experts for training sessions and incorporating continuous learning opportunities will build confidence and proficiency in users.

Broadening Access

Plans to incorporate VR into EMS must be inclusive and equitable. Efforts should aim to distribute resources such that it reaches even the most remote areas. This could include installing VR kiosks at community centers or local libraries in rural areas.

7.4. Compelling Evidence: Case Studies of VR in Disasters

Several compelling case studies underscore VR's efficacy in emergency management.

In Japan, which often experiences earthquakes, VR is used to simulate seismic activity, helping citizens rehearse evacuation drills and understand how to react during real events. This simulation not only familiarizes users with procedures but also heightens their emotional involvement, resulting in better retention of safety information.

In the United States, the Los Angeles Fire Department trained their personnel using a 180-degree VR experience, recreating the sensations of a fire in a commercial building. This intensely realistic enduring experience enabled firefighters to anticipate similar hazards and plan countering strategies.

7.5. The Future of VR in EMS

What does the future hold? As technology continues to develop, VR simulations could become even more seamless and immersive. We might see simulations that combine VR with other advancements like artificial intelligence, machine learning, and haptics to create more comprehensive training scenarios. Through continued investment and commitment, the potential impact of VR technology on emergency management is rife with opportunities.

As we progress, the focus should remain steadfast on bridging gaps and integrating VR into current emergency management systems meaningfully. As with any technology, adoption and integration should be measured, deliberate, and strategic, always keeping the ultimate goal front and center – to save lives and reduce the impacts of emergencies and disasters. The enduring commitment to this mission might well decide the future of VR's integration into emergency management systems.

Chapter 8. Masterminds Behind VR Tech: In Conversation with leading Developers

Virtual reality (VR) has been a game-changer in numerous fields, emergency management being one of them. To delve deeper into this intriguing phenomenon, let's turn our attention towards the masterminds behind it - the VR developers. Leading VR developers are constantly exploring the boundaries of this technology, pushing for more immersive, realistic experiences. But how did they integrate this technology into the landscape of emergency response tactics?

8.1. The Genesis of an Idea

The inception of integrating VR in emergency management can be traced back to the growing understanding of the power of immersive technology, according to Alex Beck, a lead developer at a cutting-edge VR tech firm. He explained, "We started to realize that VR could be used for much more than just gaming and entertainment. It could actually place people in a 'what-if' scenario, allowing them to react, make decisions, and learn."

Beck recalls the moment when the team decided to focus on emergency management. A high-profile disaster made the news, and there was criticism about the lack of preparedness. This incident prompted Beck and his team to consider utilizing VR technology as a tool for training and preparation for such emergencies.

8.2. Transforming the Idea into Reality

Turning this concept into a reality wasn't a simple task. Sophia Perry, another leading developer, recounts the arduous journey. "Building an immersive, realistic disaster scenario was a tremendous challenge," Perry recounted. "There were countless variables to consider, from the visuals and sound effects to the critical elements such as unpredictability and time pressure."

It was important to create a virtual environment that replicated real-life disasters as closely as possible. Collaboration became the key, states Perry. Developers started working closely with experts from the fields of disaster management, psychology, and even meteorology to create a comprehensive VR experience.

8.3. The Challenges and Triumphs of Development

Although the path towards creating VR programs for emergency management was riddled with obstacles, the joys from the small victories along the way were beneficial. James Reynolds, another top VR developer, shared an incident that brought the real potential of their work to light.

"There was a time when we had handed a demo version of the software we developed to a group of firefighters," Reynolds began. "They tested it, putting themselves in a virtual emergency situation. And then it clicked — they saw the value. Seeing their positive reactions made all the challenges worth it."

8.4. Responding to Market Feedback, Post Deployment

Like any other technology, VR for emergency management also had to undergo trial and error post deployment. Gathering user feedback and adapting to it is a constant process. Terry White, a dynamic veteran in the field, shared some insightful experiences.

"The responses were mixed in the beginning," White said, acknowledging the initial hesitations from emergency response units in using the novel technology. But she also observed that as they carried on with the testing and adaptation process, the reception started to change. "Once they saw the efficiency difference, the potential benefits, they started to jump on board."

8.5. The Future: Unbounded Potential

VR's potential in the emergency management realm seems unrestrained. Each developer we spoke to was filled with enthusiasm for what lies ahead. With advancements in technology, they foresee more intricate, realistic simulations that will further improve training and preparedness levels.

In summing up, Perry expressed a captivating vision. "The day isn't far when our VR programs will be a standard in emergency response training worldwide. That's the goal we're working towards," she said, a reflection of the passion and optimism felt by the developers who are the key figures within this transformational process.

This chapter provides a thoughtful road map into the backgrounds and processes behind VR's application in the field of emergency management. It explores the experiences, trials, and achievements these leading developers undergo, as they continue to unlock new potentials in VR. They are indeed the masterminds who facilitate the crucial link between innovative technology and strategic emergency preparedness.

Chapter 9. Benefits and Challenges: A Balanced Perspective on VR in Emergency Management

The rapid evolution of technology has grounded its roots in nearly every operational sphere. The same evolution has forged an integral tool in emergency management - Virtual Reality (VR). Offering immersive, realistic scenarios that extend the boundaries of training exercises and operational insights, virtual reality is revolutionizing how responders prepare for and manage emergencies.

9.1. The Benefits of VR in Emergency Management

Perhaps the most significant advantage of integrating VR into emergency management practices is the ability to provide a safe environment for training. Emergency responders can practice high-risk procedures and tricky maneuvers without a threat to their lives, allowing them to build confidence and competence in dealing with various scenarios.

For instance, they can simulate catastrophic events like earthquakes, floods, and fires, enabling response teams to train under stress-inducing conditions. These simulations can recreate entire towns, various types of architectures, and diverse weather conditions, emulating a wide range of complex disaster scenarios.

Notably, VR provides an avenue for perpetual learning. The system is structured in such a way that practitioners can repeat the training scenarios as many times as needed, reflecting on their actions, and learning from their mistakes until they achieve the desired proficiency level. This flexibility significantly speeds up the learning process, ensuring faster assimilation of response protocols.

Interoperability is one more facet where VR shines. Integration with other advanced technologies such as Artificial Intelligence (AI) makes it possible to create smart systems. These systems can adapt to the trainees' level of expertise, offering tailored training sessions that progressively challenge their skills and critical thinking capacities, an aspect crucial in the emergency response domain.

From an administrative perspective, virtual reality allows for cost-effective and efficient training. Unlike traditional physical training exercises, VR simulations don't require as many tangible resources or extensive logistics. This lean efficiency makes it increasingly possible to train higher numbers of responders with fewer funds, widening the capacity for proficient disaster management dramatically.

9.2. Challenges of Utilizing VR in Emergency Management

Despite its many advantages, VR implementation in emergency management also presents unique challenges. One of the key hurdles is the cost associated with developing tailor-made VR systems, which can be prohibitively expensive. High-end VR headsets and the computational hardware to render detailed virtual environments need substantial investment, which might not be viable for smaller or less affluent community organisations.

Moreover, customizing the VR software to replicate local geographical features and city structures accurately demands significant technical expertise, time, and financial resources. Hence, organizations must assess whether the benefits outweigh the cost and complex development process.

The physical interactions within the VR realm pose another challenge. Virtual reality simulations are more effective when they imitate real world conditions as closely as possible. However, not all physical actions can be appropriately translated into virtual actions, which might undercut the training efficacy.

One often overlooked issue is that prolonged exposure to VR scenarios can lead to motion sickness or extreme disorientation for some users, which can limit the duration of training sessions.

Moreover, while VR-based training is rigorous and consistent, it might not entirely prepare responders for the emotional stress accompanying real-life disasters. The human suffering and fear that comes with actual emergencies is challenging to simulate accurately in VR, and such lack of emotional preparedness can potentially impact the performance in real-world scenarios.

Any technology, regardless of how groundbreaking, inevitably harbors disadvantages alongside benefits. The key lies in how its users negate the negatives while capitalizing on the positives. Virtual reality for emergency management stands as no exception to this rule. It harbors the potential to massively overhaul how training and disaster response are conducted, but only if the hurdles in its path are dealt with smartly and efficiently.

9.3. Meeting the Challenges: Optimal Use of VR in Emergency Management

Addressing the challenges in utilizing VR in emergency management isn't easy, yet it's vital. Organizations need to adopt a strategic approach towards implementation, which invariably begins with a cost-benefit analysis.

Securing funding for VR projects could be realized through various channels, ranging from governmental grants to partnerships with tech firms. The key lies in effective negotiation and presenting a compelling case about the advantages VR holds for emergency management.

Collaborative funding can act as a significant enabler. Agencies can come together to share costs, design common training programs, and jointly benefit from VR systems. This would not only pool funds but also collective experience, accelerating the learning curve.

Technological advances in VR equipment that are making it more affordable and user-friendly by the day provide some reprieve, too. Furthermore, partnerships with software firms specialized in VR could bring down the technical barrier.

A phased approach to VR implementation could also be beneficial, especially for smaller organizations. Begin with off-the-shelf VR tools, then gradually move towards customized solutions as resources allow.

Partnering with academia and involving students in the development or iterative testing stages can invigorate the VR programs. Universities often have access to technical expertise and may be eager to participate in real-world applications of VR tech. This collaboration could, in turn, also reduce development costs.

From a health perspective, managing disorientation and motion sickness by designing software to include regular real-world breaks or by limiting session times could prove helpful. Additionally, preparing responders for the emotional challenges of real scenarios is essential. This preparation could involve blending traditional training methods with virtual reality training.

While the path to optimal VR implementation in emergency management is strewn with challenges, it is by no means impassable. With the right blend of strategy, collaboration, innovation, and patience, the future of VR in emergency management is incredibly bright. As the promise outweighs the struggles, continued efforts to conquer the obstacles remain a practical and deserving cause. The manifestation of a world where emergency responders virtually train to save actual lives is an incredible feat, standing testament to the harmonious unison of creative technology and unwavering human determination.

Chapter 10. Future Implications: Projecting the Growth of VR in Crisis Management

In the realm of technology and its inevitable march towards the future, few advancements show as much promise as Virtual Reality (VR). What was merely the stuff of science fiction a few decades ago, has now become a tangible, transformative tool, especially in the realm of crisis management.

10.1. The Current Landscape

At present, VR is already a key part of many branches of Emergency Management. It's being increasingly integrated into training regimens for first responders, allowing for a level of realism and engagement that traditional methods could never match. And while these current uses are compelling in and of themselves, they only scratch the surface of VR's full potential.

Consider the psychological aspect of crisis response. When confronted with a real-life disaster, even the best-trained responders can find themselves hindered by natural human reactions such as panic or shock. VR offers intriguing possibilities for acclimatizing personnel to such scenarios, improving their ability to perform under pressure.

10.2. Quantifying the Impact

The benefits of VR in crisis managerment go beyond the anecdotal. A study conducted by the University of Maryland, for example, found that people remember information better if they've learned it in a virtual environment as compared to a two-dimensional desktop. This could have substantial implications for disaster response efforts, where rapid recall of information can mean the difference between life and death.

We also shouldn't underestimate how VR's immersive capabilities encourage empathy and understanding. For decision-makers who may never have direct experience with disaster scenarios, this could be an invaluable advantage in crafting more effective responses.

10.3. A Glimpse into the Future

Looking ahead, the rise of VR in crisis management is poised for exponential growth. As the technology continues to mature, we can anticipate its further integration into all levels of the emergency management panorama, from education and training to tactical response and recovery.

In the education sector, for example, we can expect to see VR used to create even more immersive, real-world simulations to help train future crisis managers. These simulations can be designed to replicate a variety of conditions and scenarios that couldn't otherwise be safely practiced, from large-scale natural disasters to terrorist attacks.

Complementing this, we may see a rise in supplemental VR programs that target psychological training, aiming to enable responders to better handle the stresses and panic that can accompany real-life emergencies.

The tactical aspect of crisis management will also see a significant overhaul with the growth of VR technology. Imagine that during a disaster, a rescue team leader could use a VR headset to virtually visit the disaster site, getting a real-time, 360-degree view of the situation and making informed decisions without needing to be physically present.

In the recovery phase of crisis management, VR could play an equally crucial role. It could facilitate walkthroughs of disaster-struck zones, assisting in the assessment of damage and in planning rebuilds. Moreover, it could allow affected residents to navigate their reconstructed cities or neighborhoods before any actual construction begins.

10.4. Boon or Curse?

Of course, as with any technology, the expanded use of VR in crisis management comes with its own set of concerns. Key among these is the fear that relying too heavily on VR might actually reduce the efficacy of responses, as personnel might struggle to translate their virtual experiences to reality. Add to this the initial costs for implementation and maintenance, and we have several key issues that will need to be addressed.

Yet, despite these potential stumbling blocks, the promise of VR in crisis management is undeniable. As we move forward, it will be critical to balance this potential with the necessary caution and oversight, paving the way for a future where VR can be fully harnessed in managing crises more effectively than ever before.

10.5. Wrapping Up

As we survey the future landscape of VR in crisis management, one thing becomes exceedingly clear: the potential for transformation is enormous. Though challenges lie ahead, the promise of improved training, more effective responses, and enhanced recovery efforts is a compelling vision. This chapter of our journey in using technology for crisis management is only just beginning.

The VR revolution is unfolding, and as it moves forward, we must remain willing to innovate, adapt, and learn. The ultimate goal? To harness the true power of VR, transforming crisis management and bringing about a future where we can respond to disasters swiftly, effectively, and compassionally.

Chapter 11. Afterword: A World Safer with VR? Pondering the Practicality, Ethics and Future

As the final chapter of this comprehensive exploration of virtual reality in emergency management, it is appropriate that we reflect on the implications and potential future of this transformative technology. A posthumous debate invariably twines around adopting any technology, especially one as potent and pervasive as Virtual Reality.

11.1. A World Safer with Virtual Reality?

The widespread implementation of VR in disaster management, as previous chapters asserted, has myriad advantages – ranging from augmenting first-hand training experiences for emergency responders, facilitating more effective planning and preparedness, to transforming public awareness of and engagement in disaster management.

In training scenarios, VR allows emergency management personnel to immerse themselves in a gamut of contexts that duplicate actual emergency environments — hurricanes, earthquakes, floods, fires, terrorist attacks — thereby helping them hone their skills and instincts in a safe arena. Preemptive planning and tangible data representation can be made more efficient and deceptive.

Simultaneously, awareness campaigns augmented by VR can encourage the understanding of disaster-stricken circumstances, provoking empathetic responses and inducing environmentally friendly practices.

Yet, the perturbing question remains - Does implementing VR unequivocally make the world a safer place? While the benefits seem to tilt the scales positively, it is incumbent upon us to examine the shortcomings of VR technology and its conceivable backlash, which we'll discuss in the following segments.

11.2. Pondering the Practicality

In any discourse on technology's applicability, the issue of feasibility inevitably arises. Despite the exponential evolution of technology, VR is still nascent and expensive, creating a barrier to its broad-scale deployment. Not only the headsets but the computers required to run VR programs need to be high-end, slashing the feasibility for smaller organizations or developing regions with tight monetary constraints.

Moreover, the operation of VR technology requires advanced technical knowledge, further augmenting its costs as specialized training needs to be allocated for its successful operation.

Add the potential for simulation sickness, which can occur due to the dissonance between what the user perceives in the VR and the reality — leading to symptoms like dizziness, nausea, and headaches, which may deter its widespread acceptance.

11.3. Ethics of Virtual Reality

The ethical considerations of VR serve as another slippery slope. When people participate in emergency simulations, there's a risk of resurfacing trauma. Although VR provides realistic scenarios for increased effectiveness, the line between reality and fiction sometimes blurs – potentially leading to severe psychological distress.

Moreover, in the enthusiasm to exploit VR's capabilities for good, the potential for misuse by malicious actors should not be underestimated. Whether it's creating panic through misinformation or using VR technology for terrorizing purposes, the darker side of humanity could potentially exploit VR in ways that make our world more dangerous.

11.4. Future of Virtual Reality in Emergency Management

Despite these challenges, the future of VR in emergency management brims with possibility. The cost of VR technology, both hardware and software, is gradually decreasing, making it more accessible to a broader community. Developments in haptic feedback systems offer a more immersive and realistic VR experience, enhancing the effectiveness of emergency training simulations.

Moreover, advances in AI and data analysis could enable more realistic disaster simulations, with VR environments adapting in real-time to mimic the chaotic and unpredictable nature of disaster scenarios. Combining VR with other technologies such as drones and IoT could provide more detailed and accurate real-time data for disaster planning and emergency response.

While we must be prudent and reflective, it would be a folly to step back from this transformative technology that promises to revolutionize our approach towards emergency management.

This thorough analysis should not act as an overture to dissuade technology adoption but serve as a reminder of the responsibilities we hold alongside the possibilities we envision. Unsurprisingly, the road to a safer world twines with innovations and ethical considerations. Endeavoring to balance the two will ensure a future secure in the throes of disasters and emergencies.